MW00592753

HANA ZÜKI

MANY MOODS
JOURNAL

Abrams Books For Young Readers
• New York •

Cataloging-in-Publication Data has been applied for and may be
obtained from the Library of Congress.

ISBN 978-1-4197-3324-6

HASBRO and its logo HANAZUKI and all related characters are trademarks of Hasbro
and used with permission. © 2018 Hasbro. All rights reserved.

Book design by Deena Fleming

Published in 2018 by Abrams Books for Young Readers, an imprint of ABRAMS. All rights reserved. No portion of
this book may be reproduced, stored in a retrieval system, or transmitted in any form or by any means,
mechanical, electronic, photocopying, recording, or otherwise, without written permission from the publisher.
Printed and bound in U.S.A.

10 9 8 7 6 5 4 3 2 1

Abrams Books are available at special discounts when purchased in quantity for premiums and promotions as
well as fundraising or educational use. Special editions can also be created to specification. For details, contact
specialsales@abramsbooks.com or the address below.

Abrams® is a registered trademark of Harry N. Abrams, Inc.

ABRAMS The Art of Books
195 Broadway, New York, NY 10007
abramsbooks.com

My name is HANAZUKI!

I'm a Moonflower who uses the power of my moods to protect my moon and all the creatures who live here from the destructive force known only as the Big Bad.

If you had a moon full of wacky creatures to befriend and protect, what would it look like? Draw your moon below.

There are other Moonflowers in the lunaverse, and together, we help protect each other's moons. And who best to help us Moonflowers protect our moons? The most adorable little buddies! They're called Alterlings, and they help intensify each of our moods.

Miyumi and Slooths

Miyumi thinks everything is fabulous, even when it isn't.

Kiazuki and Orokos

Kiazuki is strong and independent, but she has a hard time expressing herself.

Kiyoshi and Unicorns

Kiyoshi worries about everything. It keeps him safe, but it also keeps him from taking risks.

Maroshi and Flochie

Maroshi acts all carefree and chill, but he hides his true emotions sometimes.

Who are the members of your Moonflower squad? Draw them here.

· ·

We're Moonflowers.
We're family.

Little Dreamer floats throughout the lunaverse delivering treasures to us Moonflowers. When a Moonflower feels something deeply and is honest about his or her mood, the treasure glows. When a glowing treasure is planted, it grows into a Treasure Tree! Treasure Trees protect moons and ward off the Big Bad.

Little Dreamer is a mysterious little snoozy guy.
The only thing anyone knows about him for sure is his wardrobe is FABULOUS!

Design some outfits for Little Dreamer!

COLOR IS VERY IMPORTANT IN MY WORLD!
EVERY COLOR IS CONNECTED
TO A SPECIFIC MOOD:

RED: FEISTY

RASPBERRY: HOPEFUL

PINK: LOVING

ORANGE: WACKY

YELLOW: HAPPY

GREEN: MELLOW

LIME GREEN: SCARED

EMERALD: JEALOUS

BLUE: SAD

TEAL: FABULOUS

PURPLE: COURAGEOUS

LAVENDER: INSPIRED

DO YOU THINK ANY MOODS ARE MISSING? WHAT ARE THEY? WHAT COLORS DO YOU THINK THEY WOULD BE?

RAINBOW: CREATIVE

Draw and describe your current mood.

"WE CAN'T ALL BE FEISTY ALL THE TIME. IT MAKES EVERYTHING GET A BIT TOO CRAZY. JUST A LITTLE FEISTINESS IS PLENTY." —HANAZUKI

What would you do with just a little feistiness?

....

....

....

....

....

....

....

....

....

....

....

Red Hemka is a very feisty leader. Sometimes his feistiness helps him get things done. Other times it gets him into trouble.

Make a list of qualities you think a good leader should have. Do you know someone with these qualities?

....

....

....

....

....

....

....

....

Draw their picture here!

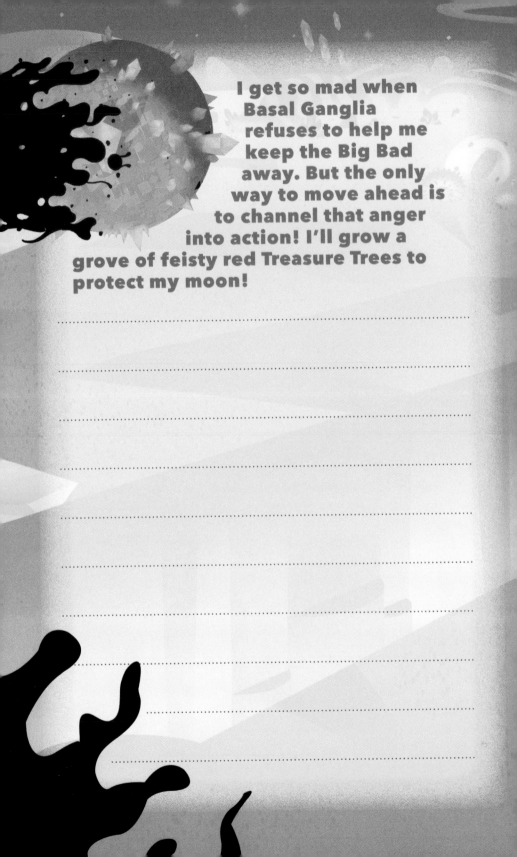

I get so mad when Basal Ganglia refuses to help me keep the Big Bad away. But the only way to move ahead is to channel that anger into action! I'll grow a grove of feisty red Treasure Trees to protect my moon!

....
....
....
....
....
....
....
....
....

Can you think of a time when being angry made you feel powerful? What are some ways you can use feisty energy for good?

Being in charge and bossing people around makes Basal Ganglia feel powerful.

What makes you feel powerful?

Write about a dream you wish would come true.

"I GUESS WE ALL DO THINGS WE REGRET.
IT'S JUST A MATTER OF HOW YOU DEAL
WITH THEM." —SLEEPY UNICORN

Have you ever regretted something? What did you do to learn from it? What will you do to avoid having regrets in the future?

When things seem grim, I hardly ever lose hope, and sometimes, Little Dreamer shows up with just the extra bit of hope I need.

What helps you feel hopeful?
Who or what helps you see that things
can always get better?

....
....
....
....
....
....
....
....
....
....
....
....
....

"Not judging myself so harshly is what allowed me to grow." —Kiazuki

What are your favorite things about yourself?

I am . . .

"HOME IS WHERE THE HEART IS, AND MY HEART IS HERE. IN MY HOME." —HANAZUKI

Draw the people you love. Design your own Moonflower Power Tower where you can all hang out!

IF YOU WERE A MOONFLOWER, WHAT WOULD YOUR ALTERLINGS BE CALLED? WHAT WOULD THEY LOOK LIKE?

I have a lot of questions about the way things work on my moon. What do you wonder about? What are your big questions about the way things work in your world?

Draw and describe your current mood.

Are you ready to get wacky?
Turn this book upside down!

One time, when I came back from a long trip, Orange let me know how happy he was to see me by doing so many backflips that he made us both dizzy! What is the silliest thing you've ever done?

I'm so excited! I can't wait to see what you come up with.

If you could do anything you wanted for a whole day, what would you do? Think BIG! Think BOLD! Stand on your head and think some more! We're talking about your perfect, anything goes, who-cares-what-anyone-else-thinks kind of day here!

....

....

....

....

....

....

....

....

....

....

Express your wacky side! Draw a
picture of an undiscovered moon
creature. And . . . go!

"Who am I?
What do I want out of all this?
What I'm trying to say is . . .
I'm hungry." —Maroshi

Just when you think you know what Maroshi is going to say, he says something totally unexpected. It makes me so happy when my friends surprise me. Write about a time when your friends made you happy.

I'm happiest when my friends and I are safe.
What makes you happiest?

....

....

....

....

....

....

....

....

....

....

....

....

....

When you're happy, it's natural to want to spread that good feeling.

What do you do to make the people you love happy, too?

"EVERYBODY'S GOT THEIR PART TO PLAY. TEAMWORK MAKES THE DREAM WORK!" —DAZZLESSENCE JONES

What talents do you have that make you a good team player?

. . . .

....

....

....

....

....

....

....

....

....

....

....

Maroshi meditates to keep himself calm.
What do you do to stay chill? Draw yourself
at your most relaxed.

"There's nothing I'd rather do than spend every day by myself, alone, in this cave." —Basal Ganglia

Sometimes it's good to spend time alone. What do you like to do when you're on your own?

"If I'm not chill . . . I don't know what I am." —Maroshi

Some people are really great at staying chill, while others need a little help finding ways to relax. How do you help others stay chill?

Mirror Plant says the things that I'm thinking but won't say out loud.

What's something that you wish you could tell your friend but you haven't yet?

What's keeping you from speaking the truth?

. . . .

....

....

....

....

....

....

....

....

....

Draw and describe your current mood.

Being anxious or scared can make it really hard for me to make a decision. What do you do when you're having a hard time trying to decide on something?

Try making a list of pros and cons to help!

Pros

Cons

Pros

Cons

When is it good for you to be afraid?

....

....

....

....

....

....

....

....

....

....

....

....

....

....

For a long time, I was afraid of the Dark Side of my moon. But once I visited, I saw that it's not so bad. And I even made a good friend—Doughy Bunington!

Write about something that frightens you. How do you get past this fear?

There is a Safety Cave on my moon where everybody goes when it's all chaos outside.

Design your own Safety Cave. What would you put in it?

My friends and I sometimes get jealous of each other. It's easy to become jealous when someone has something you want.

For a long time, Kiazuki was jealous that I was able to grow Treasure Trees on my moon, and she couldn't grow a Treasure Tree anywhere she tried. But once she realized her true mood, she was able to do it!

Has a friend ever been jealous of you?
What for, and how did you help them move
past their jealousy?

....

....

....

....

....

....

....

....

....

....

....

....

....

Everyone gets jealous once in a while. When Emerald and Raspberry Hemka spend more time with Kiazuki than they do with me, I glow emerald with envy. I just want my Hemka to be happy! And I want to hang out with the little guys, too.

Think of a time when you were envious of a friend. How did you get past it?

Doughy Bunington and his sister Hammy go to great lengths to try to impress each other.

Do you think it's important to be impressive? What makes you impressive?

. . . .

....

....

....

....

....

....

....

....

....

....

> "Brains have feelings, too, you know." —Basal Ganglia

What do you do when you're feeling blue? What do you do to make yourself feel better?

When I thought the Hemka were leaving me, I picked flowers for them from my Friendship Garden as a goodbye gift.

If your good friend was moving away, what gift would you give? Draw it!

Doughy Bunington and Chicken Plant have still not resolved their differences. Sometimes forgiveness is hard. Can you think of a time you had to forgive someone who upset you? How did you feel when they apologized?

....

....

....

....

....

....

....

....

Write about a time you upset someone you care about. What did you do to get them to forgive you?

Kiyoshi feels so bad about letting Twisted Unicorn take over his moon, he can only grow black Treasure Trees. The trees can't protect his moon from the Big Bad, but they do offer hints about the future. Sometimes, when you're having a hard time, thinking about the future can be a reminder that things will get better.

Make a list of all the good things you hope will happen in the future. Remind yourself of this list when you're feeling down!

"Everyone gets to do whatever they want! That's the secret to a truly fab-tastic life." —Miyumi

How would you make
your life truly fab-tastic?

1. ....

2. ....

3. ....

4. ....

One of the things that makes Miyumi feel so fabulous is music. What are your 10 favorite songs?

5. ....

6. ....

....

7. ....

....

8. ....

....

9. ....

....

10. ....

....

Do you agree with Miyumi? Write about
what life would be like without all the feels.

....

....

....

....

....

....

....

....

....

....

....

....

....

BEFORE I WAS A MOONFLOWER, THE OTHER MOONFLOWERS GOT TOGETHER AND FORMED A SUPERHERO SQUAD CALLED THE GARLANDIANS.

Who are the superheroes in your life?
Design costumes for your superhero squad!

WHEN THE HEMKA COME TOGETHER TO FORM RAINBOW HEMKA, ANYTHING IS POSSIBLE.

Sort of like here, on this blank page.
Fill it with anything you can imagine!

"IF YOU NEVER TAKE RISKS, YOU'LL NEVER HAVE ANY FUN! FACT!" —HANAZUKI

Being a Moonflower means that I have to be brave. Do you like taking risks? Why or why not?

Why?

....

....

....

....

Why not?

....

....

....

....

Why?

....
....
....
....

Why not?

....
....
....
....

Why?

....
....
....
....

Why not?

....
....
....
....

If you could take a Mouth Portal anywhere you wanted in your lunaverse, where would you go?

"IF YOU'RE NEVER AFRAID, YOU CAN NEVER BE BRAVE." —HANAZUKI

Write about the bravest thing you've ever done.

The black Treasure Tree forest on Kiyoshi's moon is a dark and scary place, but to Kiyoshi, it feels like home.

Can you think of a time that something that frightened you became familiar and not so scary? Or someone who frightened you at first and then became your friend?

. . . .

....

....

....

....

....

....

....

....

BEING THE HARDEST THING IN THE LUNAVERSE GIVES DAZZLESSENCE JONES A LOT OF CONFIDENCE.

What makes you feel confident?

. . . .

....

....

....

....

....

....

....

....

....

....

....

Draw the best idea you've ever had.

When I first arrived on my moon, I had to figure things out for myself. When I met the other Moonflowers, each one taught me something new.

Think of three of your friends. What have they each taught you? What have you taught them?

Enormous Coal is a little guy, but that doesn't stop him from believing he's the most powerful thing around. Draw something small that is also mighty.

> **"MAGIC IS LIKE WHEN YOU ZAP STUFF AND *POOF*, IT'S FIXED."**
> **—SLEEPY UNICORN**

What would you do if you had magical powers?

. . . .

....

....

....

....

....

....

....

....

....

....

....

....

Draw and describe your current mood.

> **"Nothing on this moon agrees with me!"** —Chicken Plant

What do you do when you're feeling out of sorts, like you don't belong?

. . . .

....

....

....

....

....

....

....

....

....

....

....

Draw and describe your current mood.

Draw the scariest monster you can imagine!

Are you ready to get wacky *again*?
Turn this book upside down!

....

....

....

....

....

....

....

....

....

....

....

Sometimes, when you look at things from a different angle, you notice something you didn't see before. Write about a time something or someone seemed to be one thing but turned out to be something different.

OH! RAINBOW HEMKA HAS FOUND ANOTHER BLANK PAGE!

What do you think should go here? Draw it!

Who's your favorite hug buddy? Grab them and give them a big squeeze! Then draw a picture of you and your hug buddy!

OR IS THIS JUST THE BEGINNING?

IS THIS THE END?